Simple Strategy to Save $1M in Retirement

My Journey that Everyone Can Follow

A guide to building financial freedom through consistent saving, simple investing, and proven strategies for everyday people.

AF800947

Hope Grace
PUBLISHING
Alexandria, Virginia, USA

By **Hope Grace**

For permission requests, please contact the publisher at the address below:
Published by Hope Grace Publishing
HopeGracePublishing.com
Alexandria, Virginia, USA

This book is a work of nonfiction. While the author has made every effort to provide accurate and up-to-date information, the content is for informational purposes only and should not be considered professional financial advice. Readers should consult with a licensed financial advisor or other qualified professional for their specific financial needs.

ISBN: 978-1-966423-17-1
Library of Congress Control Number:
2024926724

First Edition: 2025

Table of Contents

Author's Note

When I first read that only 12% of Americans have saved $1 million or more by retirement, I was astonished. I couldn't believe that such a small percentage of people had reached a milestone that seemed entirely achievable with consistent effort and a simple plan.

As I reflected on my own financial journey — from starting with nothing in my 30s to saving over $1 million for retirement — I realized that the strategies I used could benefit countless others. This book is my way of sharing what I've learned, showing you that building significant wealth is possible no matter where you're starting from.

To put it into perspective, here's how much you need to save monthly to reach $1 million by age 65, assuming an 8% annual return:

Start at 15: $95/month

Start at 25: $285/month

Start at 35: $670/month

Start at 45: $1,700/month

The earlier you start, the easier it becomes, thanks to the magic of compounding. But even if you're starting later, there's still hope. Every step forward counts, and it's never too late to begin.

I wrote this book to simplify the path to financial freedom and empower you to take control of your future. My hope is that these strategies inspire you to start saving, stay consistent, and achieve the life you've dreamed of for yourself and your loved ones.

This is your journey, and it starts today. Let's begin.

—Hope Grace

Introduction

When I arrived in the United States at the age of 30, I carried with me a degree in philosophy, big dreams, and no savings. The road ahead was uncertain, and the odds were stacked against me. Like many immigrants, I faced numerous challenges — from adapting to a new culture to finding a stable career. I took out student loans to pursue a new degree in computer studies, transitioned into a tech career, and navigated periods of unemployment and underemployment. Yet, through determination, careful planning, and consistent action, I achieved what seemed impossible: building $1 million in retirement savings.

This book is my journey — not just a story of personal triumph, but a practical guide for anyone who dreams of achieving financial freedom. You won't find complex financial jargon or risky investment schemes here. Instead, you'll discover simple, proven strategies that anyone can follow, regardless of their starting point. These are the same strategies I used to go from zero to $1 million, even while navigating layoffs, single parenthood, and a modest government salary.

Financial freedom is not about earning a six-figure income, receiving large inheritances, or having a flawless career path. It's about making smart decisions, staying consistent, and harnessing the power of time and compounding. If I could achieve this as an immigrant with a late start, so can you. My story is proof that it's never too late to take control of your financial future.

Whether you're just starting your career, facing financial setbacks, or wondering if you'll ever have enough for retirement, this book is for you. My hope is to inspire you to believe in your own ability to build a secure and comfortable future. The journey may not always be easy, but I promise you: it's worth it.

Chapter 1: Start Where You Are

When I came to the United States at the age of 30, I was starting from scratch. With a degree in philosophy, no savings, and no experience in the U.S. job market, I knew I needed to build a new foundation for my life. Going back to school felt like the right decision, but it came with its own set of challenges, including taking on student loans to fund my education. As I transitioned into a career in computer studies, I thought I was finally on my way. Then, life threw its first major curveball: I was laid off from my first full-time job after 9/11, just a year into my new career.

Finding another full-time role in IT took six long years. During that time, I was underemployed, juggling contract work while raising my child as a single mom. It wasn't easy. There were moments of doubt, stress, and financial strain. But even during those difficult years, I made the decision to prioritize saving for retirement. I understood that every dollar saved, no matter how small, had the potential to grow over time.

This decision came from a mindset that shaped my entire financial journey: **start now, no matter where you are.** It doesn't matter if you're starting late, have limited income, or are unsure about the future. What matters is taking that first step and committing to the habit of saving and investing.

One of the most important lessons I've learned is that **retirement savings should be prioritized from your very first paycheck — even if it's from a part-time summer job.** I followed this principle with my son when he worked summer jobs at Burger King. I invested all his earnings into his Roth IRA account, setting him up for a financial future he didn't yet understand. For me, starting late meant playing catch-up. But if you're younger or just beginning your career, you have the most powerful ally in investing: **time.**

Overcoming setbacks isn't just about perseverance — it's about adopting the right mindset. Whether you're starting late, recovering from financial hardships, or simply trying to figure out where to begin, the key is to focus on what you can control today. Every small step adds up, and it's never too late to get started.

Your journey begins wherever you are right now. You don't have to wait for a perfect moment, higher income, or complete understanding. Start small, start today, and trust that your consistent efforts will lead to big results. Remember: it's not about where you begin; it's about where you're heading.

Chapter 2: The Power of Consistent Savings

Saving for retirement isn't just about putting money away — it's about creating a habit that builds wealth over time. The key to success is consistency, even in the face of life's challenges. For 20 years, I maxed out my Roth IRA contributions every single year, even during the most difficult times. Whether I was underemployed, managing tight budgets as a single mom, or navigating unexpected expenses, I made retirement savings a non-negotiable priority.

The Importance of Saving Early and Often

The earlier you start saving, the more powerful your money becomes. This is thanks to the magic of **compound interest**, where your money earns returns, and then those returns earn returns. Over time, even small contributions grow into substantial amounts.

For example:

- Saving $6,000 annually in a Roth IRA starting at age 25 can grow to over $1.4 million by age 65, assuming an average 8% annual return.
- If you wait until age 35 to start saving the same amount, your total grows to just over $600,000 by 65 — a difference of nearly $800,000, even though you only contributed $60,000 less.

For someone like me, starting late meant I had to save aggressively to catch up. But no matter when you begin, consistency is what makes the difference.

The Magic of Compounding

Think of compound interest as a snowball rolling down a hill. It starts small, but with time, it grows larger and faster. To illustrate:

- In your first year, you contribute $6,000 to a Roth IRA and earn 8% interest. That $6,000 grows to $6,480.

- In year two, you add another $6,000, and now your total is $12,480, which earns 8% interest, bringing your balance to $13,478.
- Over time, the snowball effect accelerates. By year 20, your contributions and compounded returns create exponential growth.

Practical Tips for Consistent Savings

1. Automate Your Savings

Set up automatic contributions to your retirement accounts, so you don't have to think about it. This "pay yourself first" strategy ensures your savings happen before you're tempted to spend.

2. Prioritize Retirement Accounts

Start with accounts that offer the most benefit:

- **Roth IRA**: Contributions grow tax-free, and withdrawals in retirement are tax-free.
- **401(k)**: If your employer offers a match, contribute at least enough to get the full match — this is free money!

3. Live Within Your Means

To save consistently, you need to control your expenses. Track your spending, differentiate between wants and needs, and make sacrifices if necessary.

4. Increase Contributions Over Time

As your income grows, increase your retirement contributions. You don’t need to start with the maximum; what matters is beginning with something and building from there.

5. Avoid Lifestyle Inflation

Resist the temptation to upgrade your lifestyle every time your income increases. Instead, channel raises or bonuses directly into your savings.

Staying Consistent During Tough Times

Even when life throws challenges your way, staying consistent is crucial. During my hardest years — when I was underemployed and supporting my child alone — I found ways to make it work. I cut unnecessary expenses, lived frugally, and reminded myself of my long-term goals.

The power of consistent savings lies in its ability to turn small, steady actions into life-changing results. You don't need to make big sacrifices or wait for perfect conditions. Start with what you can, stay the course, and let time and compounding do the heavy lifting. Every dollar you save today is a step closer to the financial freedom you deserve.

Conclusion: The Two Most Important Takeaways

If there's one thing you take away from this chapter, it's this: maximize your Roth IRA contributions and always contribute enough to your 401(k) to get the full employer match.

1. Maximize Your Roth IRA Contributions

The Roth IRA is one of the most powerful tools for building wealth because your money grows tax-free, and you can withdraw it tax-free in retirement.

It's especially beneficial for those who expect to be in a higher tax bracket later in life. Make it a priority to contribute the maximum allowed each year, if possible.

2. Don't Miss Free Money from Your Employer

Employer matching contributions for a 401(k) are essentially free money — something no one should leave on the table. Even if you're starting small, always contribute at least the amount required to get the full match. It's an instant return on your investment, in addition to the long-term growth of your contributions.

These two simple strategies form the foundation of consistent and effective savings. They're not complicated or risky — they're tried-and-true methods that anyone can implement. By focusing on these priorities, you'll take a giant leap toward achieving financial freedom.

Chapter 3: Investing Made Simple

Investing doesn't have to be complicated or intimidating. In fact, keeping it simple is one of the most effective strategies for building long-term wealth. When you focus on low-cost, reliable investments and stick to your plan, you eliminate the stress of constantly monitoring the market or worrying about short-term fluctuations.

Why Index Funds Work

Index funds, such as the Vanguard 500, are designed to track the performance of a broad market index like the S&P 500. They offer diversification by investing in hundreds of companies at once and come with much lower fees than actively managed funds.

Here's the key: **80% of professional financial advisors and fund managers underperform the market.** Despite their expertise and access to tools, most cannot consistently beat the returns of an index fund. Why? Because high fees, frequent trading, and market timing often eat into their returns.

For ordinary investors, this means one thing: **index funds are your best bet.** They provide solid returns over time, require minimal management, and don't rely on you — or anyone else — trying to outsmart the market.

My Investment Philosophy

My approach to investing has always been straightforward:

1. Stick to low-cost index funds
   They're predictable, efficient, and proven to deliver strong long-term returns.

2. Don't try to time the market
   No one can consistently predict market highs and lows. Jumping in and out of the market often leads to missed opportunities and lower returns.

3. Invest for the long term

   Patience is key. Market fluctuations are normal, but over decades, the trend has always been upward.

The Golden Rule: Never Pull Money Out

One of the biggest mistakes investors make is panicking during market downturns and pulling their money out. This locks in losses and prevents your investments from recovering when the market rebounds.

To put it into perspective:

- During the 2008 financial crisis, the S&P 500 dropped by over 50%. Many investors panicked and sold their investments at a loss.
- By 2013, the market had not only recovered but reached new record highs. Those who stayed invested saw their portfolios bounce back and grow even more.

The historical trend is clear: **the market always recovers over time.** Staying invested during crashes is challenging, but it's the single most important **lesson** for long-term success.

How to Get Started

1. Set Up Your Accounts

- Open a **Roth IRA** for tax-free growth and withdrawals in retirement.
- If you're employed, enroll in your company's **401(k)** plan, especially if they offer a match.

2. Understand Expense Ratios and Fees

- Always choose funds with low expense ratios. An index fund like Vanguard 500 often has expense ratios as low as 0.03%, compared to 1% or more for actively managed funds.
- Even small differences in fees can have a huge impact on your returns over time.

3. Use Automatic Contributions

- Automate your contributions to ensure consistency. Set up recurring transfers to your

Roth IRA or payroll deductions for your 401(k). This way, saving becomes a habit, and you don't have to think about it.

4. Choose Your Investments

- **Start with a simple, diversified portfolio.** A low-cost index fund that tracks the S&P 500 is an excellent foundation for your retirement investments. This fund provides exposure to a wide range of large U.S. companies and is a reliable, time-tested choice for consistent long-term growth.
- **Additional diversification?** While diversification beyond the S&P 500 can be appealing, it's important to make informed decisions based on your financial goals and risk tolerance. We'll explore these choices in more detail in the next chapter, where I'll provide guidance on selecting the best investments for your retirement portfolio.

For now, focus on getting started with a straightforward, low-cost option like the S&P 500 index fund. Remember, simplicity is key when beginning your investment journey. More nuanced strategies can come later, and I'll guide you through those in the following chapter.

Conclusion: Simplicity Wins

Investing doesn't have to be complicated to be effective. By focusing on low-cost index funds, staying invested for the long term, and avoiding the temptation to time the market, you set yourself up for success. The key is to keep it simple, consistent, and focused on your long-term goals.

Anyone can invest, regardless of income level or experience. Start today, stick to your plan, and let time and compounding work their magic. Remember: the simpler your strategy, the better your results.

Chapter 4: How to Choose Investments

Investing can feel overwhelming, especially with so many options available. However, when it comes to retirement savings, the best approach is often the simplest: stick to U.S. index funds and avoid unnecessary complexity. This chapter will guide you through the reasoning behind these choices and help you make confident decisions.

Why Stick with U.S. Index Funds?

The U.S. stock market has consistently outperformed global markets over the long term. It is home to some of the most innovative and profitable companies in the world. Investing in U.S. index funds ensures that you're participating in the growth of these businesses and benefiting from the strength and stability of the U.S. economy.

Options like the S&P 500 index fund or a total stock market index fund provide excellent diversification across hundreds (or thousands) of companies, minimizing risk while maximizing growth potential. These funds are designed to grow with the economy and offer reliable returns over time.

The Case Against Bonds, Fixed Income, and Balanced Funds

Retirement savings are long-term investments, and history has shown that the stock market always bounces back from downturns. Bonds, fixed income, money market, and balanced funds have their place in short-term investing or for those who need a steady income within the next few years. However, if you're saving for retirement and don't need to access the money for at least two years, these options can limit your growth potential.

Here's why:

- **Lower Returns**: Bonds and fixed-income investments generally offer lower returns compared to stocks. Over decades, this can result in significantly less wealth.

- **Missed Opportunities**: By allocating funds to conservative investments too early, you miss out on the higher returns that stocks provide.
- **Market Recovery is Faster Than Ever**: Historically, the U.S. stock market has rebounded from downturns in five years or less. In recent years, recovery times have shortened to as little as two years. Staying fully invested in stocks allows you to take full advantage of these rebounds.

Recommended Investment Options

1. The S&P 500 Index Fund

- This fund tracks the performance of the 500 largest companies in the U.S., offering exposure to a wide range of industries.
- It's simple, reliable, and has consistently delivered strong returns over time.

2. Total Stock Market Index Fund

- This fund includes not only the largest companies but also mid-size and small companies in the U.S. market.
- It provides even broader diversification while maintaining the benefits of a low-cost index fund.

3. For Those Interested in Trends

- If you have a strong interest in financial trends, consider adding trending index funds to your portfolio. For example, technology-focused funds are particularly appealing now due to advancements in AI and digital currencies.
- However, this is optional. For most people, sticking to the first two options (S&P 500 and total stock market funds) is sufficient.

The Key Takeaway

When it comes to retirement savings, the best approach is to invest 100% in U.S. stocks through index funds like the S&P 500 or a total stock market fund. Avoid bonds, fixed-income investments, and balanced funds unless you anticipate needing the money within the next two years.

Simplicity is your best friend in investing. Stick with proven strategies, stay consistent, and trust that the market will work in your favor over the long term. By focusing on these core principles, you'll set yourself up for a financially secure retirement.

Chapter 5: Staying on the Course

Investing isn't just about numbers — it's also about mindset. Patience and discipline often matter more than market knowledge or timing. Even the best investment plan can fail if emotions take over during challenging times. The key to long-term success is staying the course, especially during market downturns.

The Psychology of Investing

When the market is thriving, it's easy to feel confident about your investments. But when the market drops, fear and uncertainty can cloud judgment. Many investors panic, sell their assets, and lock in losses during these moments.

Successful investing requires emotional resilience. You need to understand that:

- **Market volatility is normal**: Fluctuations are part of the process, not a signal to change your strategy.

- **Time heals most losses**: Over decades, markets have consistently trended upward despite short-term crashes.

Patience and discipline are your strongest allies. Trusting your plan and resisting emotional decisions will ultimately lead to greater success than trying to "outsmart" the market.

Weathering Market Downturns

I've experienced multiple market crashes during my investing journey, including the dot-com bubble and the 2008 financial crisis. Each time, I stayed the course, trusting that the market would recover — and it did. Those who stayed invested during these downturns saw their portfolios not only rebound but grow to new heights.

However, during the most recent downturn in 2022, I made a mistake. Influenced by pessimism about America's future and widespread predictions of an impending market crash, I allowed fear to take over. I pulled my investments out, believing I was protecting my savings.

This decision wasn't grounded in facts or a long-term perspective — it was driven by emotion and uncertainty. Unfortunately, by the time I realized my mistake and returned to the market in mid-November 2024, I had missed out on significant recovery gains.

The Lesson Learned

This experience reinforced a crucial lesson for me: **even the most disciplined investors are vulnerable to emotional decisions, and these decisions can be costly.** It's easy to let fear or external narratives influence your actions, but the consequences can undermine years of progress.

Despite this misstep, my 10-year return remains over 10% because of the many years I stayed committed to a long-term strategy. This proves two important points:

1. **Mistakes are not the end of the road**: You can recover and still achieve your goals as long as you return to your plan.

2. **Staying invested works**: My earlier consistency allowed me to weather this mistake without derailing my financial journey.

Sharing This to Help You

I debated whether to include this story in the book, but I decided it was important. Why? Because it shows that even seasoned investors make mistakes, and those mistakes can serve as valuable lessons for others.

Here's what I hope you take away from my experience:

- **Don't let fear dictate your decisions**: Predictions of doom and gloom are often exaggerated and rarely accurate.
- **Trust the long-term process**: The market's resilience is well-documented. Pulling out during downturns almost always leads to missing the recovery.
- **Learn from setbacks and move forward**: Mistakes don't define your journey — what you do next does.

Even when you falter, the principles of staying the course, focusing on long-term goals, and trusting the market remain your strongest allies. I hope my story helps you avoid the same pitfall and reinforces your confidence to stay invested, no matter what challenges arise.

Tips to Avoid Emotional Decisions

1. Focus on Long-Term Goals

- Remember why you're investing in the first place: to build a secure future. Retirement is years, if not decades, away. Short-term market movements don't matter in the grand scheme of things.
- Keep your eyes on the prize, and remind yourself that temporary losses are just part of the journey.

2. Ignore the Noise

- The media often sensationalizes market drops, which can amplify fear. Avoid constantly checking the news or your portfolio during volatile times.

- Stay informed, but filter out information that doesn't align with your long-term strategy.

3. Automate Your Investments

- Automatic contributions keep you on track and prevent emotional decision-making. When your investments happen on autopilot, you're less likely to second-guess your choices.

4. Trust the Process

- Historical data shows that markets recover and grow over time. Trust the proven process of compounding and long-term investing.

5. Have a Plan for Crashes

- Before the market drops, decide how you'll react. Committing to staying invested — even writing it down — can help you avoid impulsive decisions when emotions run high.

The Key Takeaway

Staying on the course is about keeping a steady hand, even when the market feels uncertain. It's natural to feel fear during downturns, but acting on that fear can derail your progress. By focusing on your long-term goals, ignoring short-term noise, and trusting in the resilience of the market, you'll position yourself for success.

The road to financial freedom isn't without bumps, but patience and discipline will get you to the finish line. Remember: the only way to truly lose in investing is to give up. Stay invested, stay calm, and stay the course.

Chapter 6: Maximizing Employer Benefits

One of the simplest yet most powerful ways to accelerate your retirement savings is to take full advantage of your employer's 401(k) match. It's essentially free money — an opportunity no one should leave on the table. Maximizing this benefit is a small step that leads to big rewards over time.

The Importance of Employer Matches

When my son got his first full-time job after college, he didn't see the value of contributing to his retirement account. Like many young people, he felt retirement was too far away to worry about. But I insisted that he invest at least 5% of his salary, enough to get the full match his employer offered. Though he reluctantly agreed, he's now grateful for that decision and understands the importance of starting early.

Why is the employer match so important? Here's how it works:

- Employers often match your 401(k) contributions up to a certain percentage of your salary. For example, if your employer offers a 100% match on the first 5% you contribute, investing 5% doubles your savings instantly.
- That match is essentially a 100% return on your investment right from the start — something you can't get anywhere else.

How This Applies to You

If your employer offers a 401(k) match, make it your top priority to contribute at least enough to get the full match. Even if your budget is tight or you feel hesitant about investing, this is a non-negotiable step. Here's why:

1. It's Free Money

- Every dollar your employer contributes is extra savings you don't have to earn. It's a guaranteed return on your investment.

2. It Accelerates Growth

- Employer contributions, combined with your own, grow exponentially over time through compounding. The more you invest early, the greater the impact.

3. It's Easy to Start

- Contributing enough to get the full match doesn't require maxing out your 401(k). Even a small percentage of your salary can lead to significant long-term benefits.

Long-Term Benefits of Employer Contributions

To see the power of employer matching, let's look at an example:

- Assume you earn $50,000 annually, and your employer matches 100% of the first 5% you contribute. If you contribute $2,500 (5%), your employer adds another $2,500.
- Over 30 years, assuming an 8% annual return, that $5,000 yearly investment grows to over

$622,000. Without the match, it would only grow to $311,000 — a difference of $311,000!

This example illustrates how employer contributions effectively double your savings, significantly increasing your retirement nest egg.

Make It a Priority

Maximizing your employer's match is one of the easiest and most effective ways to boost your retirement savings. If you're not sure how much your employer matches, check your 401(k) plan details or speak with your HR department. Once you know, set your contributions to at least that amount.

If you're tempted to contribute less because of immediate financial pressures, remember that this is free money you're leaving behind. Even if you can't save beyond the match right now, securing the full employer contribution is a crucial first step.

The Key Takeaway

Employer matching is one of the best benefits of a 401(k) plan, and it's an opportunity no one should miss. By contributing enough to get the full match, you're doubling your investment right away and setting yourself up for long-term success. Small decisions today lead to significant rewards tomorrow, and maximizing your employer benefits is one of the easiest ways to build a financially secure future.

Chapter 7: Teaching the Next Generation

One of the greatest gifts you can give your children is a strong financial foundation. Helping them understand the value of saving and investing early can set them up for lifelong success. As parents, we often focus on providing for our children in the present, but teaching them to build wealth for the future is just as important.

Investing My Son's Summer Earnings

When my son was in high school, he spent his summer breaks working at Burger King. Instead of letting those earnings sit in a regular savings account, I invested the entire amount into his Roth IRA each year. At the time, he didn't fully understand the benefits of this decision, but I knew that starting early was key to maximizing his financial growth.

Years later, after he graduated from college and found his first full-time job, I encouraged him to continue investing. Like many young adults, he wasn't enthusiastic about contributing to retirement, but I insisted he invest at least 5% to get his full employer match. Reluctantly, he agreed, and now, as he's matured, he's thankful for the advice. He sees the value of those early investments and the discipline that came with them.

This experience taught me that as parents, we have a responsibility to guide our children financially, even before they understand the importance of these decisions.

Why Parents Should Make Financial Decisions Early

Time is the best ally in investing, and starting early makes a tremendous difference. When children begin investing at a young age, even small contributions have decades to grow through compounding. For example:

- Investing $1,000 at age 15 can grow to nearly $21,700 by age 65, assuming an 8% annual return.

- Waiting until age 30 to invest that same $1,000 results in just $10,900 by age 65 — half the amount, even though the same initial contribution was made.

Children don't always have the knowledge or foresight to prioritize saving and investing, which is why parents must step in. Responsible parenting means making decisions today that will benefit your children for a lifetime.

Actionable Advice for Parents

1. Open a Custodial Account or Roth IRA for Minors

- If your child has earned income from a job, they're eligible to contribute to a Roth IRA. As a parent, you can open a custodial Roth IRA for them and manage the account until they're old enough to take over.
- Contributions grow tax-free, and withdrawals in retirement are also tax-free, making the Roth

IRA a powerful tool for long-term wealth building.

2. Teach Basic Financial Principles

- Start with the basics: Explain how saving and investing work, the concept of compound interest, and why it's important to start early.
- Use simple examples to illustrate how their money can grow over time.

3. Lead by Example

- Share your own financial journey and the lessons you've learned. When children see you prioritizing savings and investing, they're more likely to adopt those habits themselves.

4. Involve Them in the Process

- Let your children help choose investments for their accounts, such as low-cost index funds. Involving them in the process makes it more engaging and teaches them valuable skills.

The Key Takeaway

As parents, we have the power to shape our children’s financial future. By helping them start early, teaching them the basics, and guiding them toward smart decisions, we equip them with the tools they need for lifelong success.

It’s never too early to teach the next generation the value of saving and investing. With a little effort today, you can give your children a head start that will benefit them for decades to come. After all, the best time to start investing was yesterday. The second-best time is today.

Chapter 8: Eliminating Debt

Debt can feel like a heavy burden, but managing it effectively is key to achieving financial freedom. While eliminating high-interest debt like credit cards is absolutely essential, handling lower-interest debts, such as student loans or mortgages, requires a more strategic approach.

My Journey to Paying Off Student Loans

When I first came to the U.S., I took out student loans to pursue a new career in computer studies. Carrying that debt weighed on me emotionally, even though it was at a relatively low interest rate. I prioritized paying off my student loans before maximizing my 401(k) contributions because I simply couldn't stand the thought of having that debt hanging over me.

In hindsight, this wasn't the most financially optimal choice. With low interest rates, I could have invested more in my 401(k) and likely earned a higher return over time. However, personal finance is just that — personal. For me, the peace of mind that came with eliminating my student loans was worth the trade-off.

Balancing Debt Repayment and Investing

When deciding whether to pay off debt or invest, it's important to consider several factors:

1. The Interest Rate

- **High-Interest Debt (e.g., credit cards)**: Always prioritize paying off credit card debt as quickly as possible. The interest rates on these accounts often exceed 20%, far outpacing the returns you'd earn from investing.
- **Low-Interest Debt (e.g., student loans or mortgages)**: If the interest rate on your debt is lower than the expected return from investing (typically 8% for the stock market), it often makes sense to invest instead of aggressively paying off the debt.

2. Your Emotional Comfort Level

- Some people, like me, prefer to pay off debt even if it's not the optimal financial choice. If carrying debt causes stress or anxiety, it's okay to prioritize paying it off for the sake of your mental well-being.

3. Your Financial Goals

- Strike a balance between eliminating debt and saving for the future. For example, contribute enough to your 401(k) to get the full employer match while paying down debt. This way, you're tackling both priorities at once.

Strategies for Managing Debt While Saving for Retirement

1. Eliminate Credit Card Debt First

- Focus on paying off high-interest credit card balances before investing or saving. These debts grow quickly and can derail your financial progress.

- Use methods like the **snowball** (pay off the smallest balances first) or **avalanche** (tackle the highest-interest debts first) approaches to create momentum.

2. Contribute to Retirement While Paying Off Debt

- Even if you're focused on debt repayment, don't completely neglect your retirement savings. Contributing enough to get your employer's 401(k) match ensures you're not leaving free money on the table.

3. Refinance or Consolidate Debt

- If you have high-interest loans, consider refinancing or consolidating them into a loan with a lower interest rate. This can reduce your monthly payments and free up money for saving or investing.

4. Set Clear Priorities

- Create a plan that balances debt repayment and investing. For example:

- Pay off high-interest debt aggressively.
- Contribute to your 401(k) to get the full employer match.
- Pay off moderate-interest debt while gradually increasing your retirement contributions.

5. Live Within Your Means

- Avoid accumulating new debt by living below your income. Stick to a budget, track your expenses, and resist lifestyle inflation.

The Key Takeaway

Debt repayment is an essential part of financial freedom, but it's not a one-size-fits-all decision. Eliminating high-interest debt like credit cards is non-negotiable, while low-interest debt requires a more thoughtful approach. Balancing debt repayment with investing ensures you're building for the future while freeing yourself from financial burdens.

Remember, personal finance is about what works for you. Whether you prioritize paying off debt for peace of mind or take a more strategic approach, the key is to stay consistent and focused on your long-term goals.

Chapter 9: Financial Freedom Through Simplicity

When it comes to building wealth and securing your financial future, simplicity is your best ally. You don't need complex strategies, insider knowledge, or access to exclusive investment opportunities. In fact, most people achieve success by following a straightforward plan and staying consistent.

Why Ordinary People Don't Need Complex Financial Strategies

The financial world can seem overwhelming, with endless options for investments, tools, and strategies. But the truth is, most of this complexity isn't necessary for the average person. A simple plan that focuses on proven, long-term strategies is far more effective — and easier to follow — than chasing complicated solutions.

Consider this: The vast majority of professional fund managers, with all their resources and expertise, fail to outperform simple index funds. If the experts can't consistently beat the market, why should you try?

The Pitfalls of Chasing "Hot" Investments or Bad Advice

Many investors get caught up in the excitement of the latest "hot" investment, whether it's a trending stock, cryptocurrency, or some other speculative opportunity. While these might offer short-term gains, they often come with high risks and can lead to significant losses.

Other common pitfalls include:

- **Listening to bad advice**: Be wary of tips from friends, social media, or so-called "experts" who promise quick riches.
- **Overcomplicating your portfolio**: Adding unnecessary investments can dilute returns and make managing your finances more stressful.
- **Reacting to market hype or fear**: Emotional decisions often lead to buying at the top or

selling at the bottom — both of which hurt your long-term goals.

The best way to avoid these traps is to stick to a simple, time-tested plan.

Keeping It Simple: The Path to Financial Freedom

1. Index Funds Are Your Best Friend

- Low-cost index funds, like the Vanguard S&P 500 or total stock market index funds, provide diversification and consistent returns over time.
- They require minimal management and eliminate the need to pick individual stocks or beat the market.

2. Low Fees, High Returns

- Focus on investments with low expense ratios. High fees can erode your returns over time, even if the performance seems promising in the short term.

- A difference of just 1% in fees can cost you hundreds of thousands of dollars over a lifetime.

3. Steady Contributions Win the Race

- Invest consistently, regardless of market conditions. Automate your contributions to ensure regularity and reduce the temptation to time the market.
- The strategy of dollar-cost averaging — investing a fixed amount regularly — smooths out the impact of market volatility and builds wealth steadily.

4. Stay the Course

- Avoid making frequent changes to your portfolio. Stick with your chosen plan, even during market downturns, and trust the long-term process.
- Remember, wealth is built over decades, not days.

The Key Takeaway

Financial freedom doesn't require complex strategies or risky bets. Simplicity is the foundation of success: index funds, low fees, and consistent contributions. By avoiding the distractions of hot trends and bad advice, you can focus on what truly works.

The simpler your plan, the easier it is to follow — and the greater your chances of achieving your financial goals. Trust the process, stick to the basics, and let time and consistency do the heavy lifting.

Chapter 10: Tailoring Financial Strategies to Your Stage of Life

Financial strategies are not one-size-fits-all. Your approach to saving, investing, and managing money should evolve based on your stage of life. This chapter will help you understand essential financial terms, tailor your strategy to your unique situation, and visualize what it takes to reach your goals.

Understanding Key Financial Terms

1. Compound Interest

- The interest earned on both your original investment and the interest it has already accumulated. Over time, compounding accelerates your growth, making it critical to start as early as possible.

2. Expense Ratio

- The annual fee charged by a fund as a percentage of your investment. Lower expense ratios mean more of your money stays invested. For example, an expense ratio of 0.03% is far better than 1.0%, which can cost thousands over time.

3. Asset Allocation

- The mix of investments in your portfolio (e.g., stocks, bonds, cash). For most investors, index funds offer all the diversification needed, spreading your risk across hundreds or thousands of companies.

Strategies for Different Life Stages

1. Young Professionals (20s and 30s)

- **Priority**: Take advantage of compounding by starting as early as possible.
- **Key Actions**:
    - Open a Roth IRA and contribute as much as you can each year.

    - Contribute to your 401(k) to get the full employer match.
    - Pay off high-interest debt and build an emergency fund.
- **Advice**: At this stage, investing 100% in stocks through index funds is ideal since you have time to recover from market downturns.

2. Mid-Career (40s and 50s)

- **Priority**: Catch up if you started late or maximize contributions as income grows.
- **Key Actions**:
    - Max out contributions to both your 401(k) and Roth IRA.
    - Take advantage of catch-up contributions if you're 50 or older.
    - Avoid lifestyle inflation — channel raises or bonuses into savings instead.
- **Advice**: Stay invested in stocks for long-term growth but ensure your emergency fund is robust to handle life's surprises.

3. Near-Retirees (60s and Beyond)

- **Priority**: Transition from wealth accumulation to preservation and income generation.
- **Key Actions**:
    - Adjust your asset allocation if necessary. While stocks should remain a significant part of your portfolio, you might add bonds for short-term needs.
    - Develop a withdrawal strategy to minimize taxes and ensure your savings last.
    - Delay Social Security benefits if possible to increase your monthly payouts.
- **Advice**: Continue contributing if you're still earning, but shift your focus to enjoying the freedom your financial planning has created.

Specific Retirement Calculations

Here's how much you need to save monthly to reach $1M by age 65, assuming an 8% annual return:

- **Start at 15**: $95/month
- **Start at 25**: $285/month
- **Start at 35**: $670/month
- **Start at 45**: $1,700/month

This illustrates the power of starting early. The longer you wait, the more you'll need to save each month to achieve the same goal.

The Key Takeaway

Tailoring your financial strategy to your stage of life ensures that your efforts are aligned with your current needs and future goals. Whether you're just starting out, catching up, or approaching retirement, it's never too late — or too early — to make smart decisions.

Understanding basic financial concepts, sticking to proven strategies, and adjusting as your circumstances change will set you on the path to a secure and fulfilling future. Remember, it's not about perfection — it's about persistence and progress.

Chapter 11: Action Plan for Readers

Building wealth can feel overwhelming, but with a clear, step-by-step plan, it becomes manageable and achievable. In this chapter, I'll provide you with a practical guide to start your journey toward financial freedom.

Step 1: Open a Retirement Account

The first step is to set up a retirement account if you haven't already. Depending on your situation, consider:

- **Roth IRA**: Offers tax-free growth and withdrawals in retirement. Perfect for individuals with earned income who meet the income limits.
- **401(k)**: If your employer offers a 401(k) plan, take advantage of it, especially if they provide a matching contribution.

- **Combination**: If possible, contribute to both. Maximize your Roth IRA first, then add to your 401(k) to at least get the full employer match.

Step 2: Set Up Automatic Contributions

Automation is key to consistency. By setting up automatic contributions:

- You ensure that a portion of your income is invested regularly, regardless of market conditions.
- You reduce the temptation to spend the money elsewhere.

Most 401(k) plans allow payroll deductions, while Roth IRAs can be funded through automatic transfers from your bank account.

Step 3: Choose a Low-Cost Index Fund

When it comes to my own investments, I've kept things simple and effective. My 401(k) plan is the **Thrift Savings Plan (TSP)**, a retirement savings program for federal employees. Within the TSP, I've chosen to invest entirely in the **C Fund**, which tracks the S&P 500 index. This fund provides broad exposure to large U.S. companies, consistent returns, and low fees — everything you need to build long-term wealth.

If your employer offers a 401(k) or a similar retirement plan, check if they have options like the C Fund. Index funds like these are an excellent foundation for your portfolio.

These funds:

- Provide broad diversification with exposure to hundreds or thousands of companies.
- Are cost-effective, with low expense ratios that maximize your returns.

Avoid overly complicated portfolios or high-fee funds. Simplicity is both effective and easy to manage.

Step 4: Stick to the Plan

Market downturns and economic uncertainties can tempt you to make emotional decisions, like pulling out your investments. Remember:

- **Stay invested**: The market has always recovered over time.
- **Focus on the long term**: Your goal is decades away. Short-term volatility is irrelevant in the grand scheme.
- **Trust the process**: Consistent investing and compounding will work in your favor.

Step 5: Review and Adjust Contributions as Income Increases

As your income grows, increase your contributions to retirement accounts.

- Start by maxing out your Roth IRA if you haven't already.
- Aim to increase your 401(k) contributions to the annual maximum allowed.
- If you receive a raise or bonus, allocate a portion of it directly to your investments.

Tools and Resources

To make your journey easier, leverage the following tools and resources:

- **Websites**:
    - Vanguard: Learn about index funds and open accounts.
    - Fidelity: Another great platform for retirement accounts and low-cost funds.
    - Morningstar: Research and compare funds.
- **Books**:
    - *The Simple Path to Wealth* by JL Collins: A straightforward guide to financial independence.
    - *Your Money or Your Life* by Vicki Robin: A classic on managing money and achieving financial freedom.
- **Calculators**:

- Retirement savings calculator: Available on financial websites to project your future savings.
- Compound interest calculator: Shows how your investments grow over time.

The Key Takeaway

Building wealth is not about luck or complexity — it's about following a clear, consistent plan. By taking these actionable steps, you're laying the foundation for a secure financial future.

The tools are within your reach, and the process is simpler than it seems. Start today, trust the plan, and watch as your efforts compound into lasting financial freedom.

Chapter 12: Overcoming Excuses and Challenges

Everyone has doubts when it comes to investing. Whether it's fear of starting too late, feeling like you don't earn enough, or being intimidated by financial jargon, these barriers can prevent you from taking action. The truth is, overcoming these challenges is simpler than it seems — and it starts with believing that you can succeed.

Addressing Common Fears

1. "It's Too Late"

- Many people believe they've missed their chance to save for retirement, but that's simply not true. While starting early gives you more time to benefit from compounding, starting later still makes a difference. Every dollar you save today will grow and help secure your future.
- I started building my retirement savings in my 30s after coming to the U.S. with no savings,

and I've still managed to save over $1 million. It's never too late to begin.

2. "I Don't Make Enough"

- Saving for retirement doesn't require a high income — it requires consistency. Start small, even if it's just $50 a month, and increase your contributions as your income grows.
- During my toughest years, I was underemployed as a single mom, but I still prioritized maxing out my Roth IRA. Even small contributions add up over time.

3. "I Don't Understand Investing"

- Investing can feel intimidating, but you don't need to be an expert to succeed. Stick to simple, proven strategies like investing in low-cost index funds. Let the market work for you over the long term.
- You don't need to know everything to get started. The key is to take the first step and learn as you go.

Real-Life Examples of Overcoming Obstacles

1. Starting With Nothing

I arrived in the U.S. at age 30 with no savings and took on student loans to pursue a new career. Despite setbacks like being laid off and years of underemployment, I never gave up on my goal of building financial security.

2. Staying Consistent Through Challenges

During the 2008 financial crisis, I stayed invested even as the market dropped by over 50%. That decision allowed me to benefit from the recovery and grow my savings significantly.

3. Learning From Mistakes

In 2022, I made the mistake of pulling out my investments due to pessimism about the market. While it set me back temporarily, I learned the importance of staying the course and quickly returned to my long-term strategy.

These experiences show that no matter where you start or what challenges you face, it's possible to build wealth with determination and discipline.

Encouragement to Start Now

If you've been hesitating to start saving or investing, let me remind you: **It's never too late, and it's never too early.** Whether you're in your 20s, 40s, or 60s, taking action today can make a difference in your financial future.

Start small, stay consistent, and focus on what you can control. Don't let fear or doubt hold you back. Every step you take — no matter how small — brings you closer to financial freedom.

Remember, the most successful investors aren't those who start perfectly or never make mistakes. They're the ones who start, stay the course, and keep learning along the way.

Learning From My Mistakes

Over the years, I've made my fair share of mistakes — not only in timing the market but also in choosing what to invest in. Like many new investors, I made decisions based on emotions, trends, or incomplete knowledge. However, every mistake was a lesson, and those lessons have shaped the simple, effective strategies I've shared in this book.

The beauty of learning from someone else's experience is that you don't have to repeat the same mistakes. I've laid out everything I've learned — what worked, what didn't, and how to avoid the pitfalls that can derail your financial journey. By following this plan, you can skip the trial-and-error phase and start building wealth with confidence.

The Key Takeaway

Excuses and challenges are normal, but they don't have to define your financial journey. By addressing your fears, learning from obstacles, and taking action, you can take control of your financial future.

The best time to start was yesterday. The second-best time is today. Don't wait for the perfect moment — begin now, and let the power of time, consistency, and perseverance work in your favor.

Chapter 13: Reflecting on the Journey

Reaching $1 million in retirement savings has been a deeply rewarding milestone — not just for the financial security it provides, but for the lessons learned along the way. This journey has taught me the value of discipline, resilience, and simplicity, and I'm filled with gratitude for the opportunities that made it possible.

Gratitude and Lessons Learned

Looking back, I'm thankful for the challenges I faced. They forced me to grow, adapt, and persevere. Coming to the U.S. at 30 with no savings, taking on student loans, and navigating career setbacks weren't easy, but they shaped my determination. I learned:

The power of starting, no matter how late

- Even small steps can lead to big results over time.

The importance of patience and discipline

- Staying consistent, even in the face of uncertainty, was critical to my success.

The value of simplicity

- By focusing on low-cost index funds and avoiding unnecessary risks, I built wealth without stress or complexity.

Reaching this point wasn't about luck or privilege — it was about sticking to a plan, making sacrifices when necessary, and believing in the long-term process.

Encouragement for Readers

If there's one thing I want you to take away from this book, it's this: **You can achieve financial freedom, too.** It doesn't matter where you're starting from — what matters is your willingness to begin and stay the course.

Maybe you're starting late, like I did, or feel like you don't earn enough to save. Perhaps you're overwhelmed by the idea of investing. Whatever your situation, know this:

- It's never too late to start.
- You don't need to be perfect or wealthy to succeed.
- Every step forward, no matter how small, brings you closer to your goals.

I wrote this book to show you that financial freedom is within your reach. By learning from my mistakes and following the strategies I've shared, you can create a secure and fulfilling future for yourself and your loved ones.

A Vision for the Future

Financial freedom is about more than just numbers — it's about what that freedom allows you to do. For me, it means living comfortably in retirement, free from financial stress. It also means being able to pass on not just wealth, but the knowledge and habits that made it possible.

I want to empower the next generation to start early, stay consistent, and build a strong financial foundation. Whether it's teaching my son about investing or sharing my journey with you, I believe in the power of passing on these lessons.

Your journey doesn't end with achieving financial freedom — it's the beginning of a new chapter where you can enjoy the fruits of your labor and inspire others to do the same.

The Key Takeaway

This journey has been one of growth, learning, and persistence. It's proof that no matter where you start or what challenges you face, financial freedom is possible.

I hope my story has shown you that you're capable of reaching your goals, too. The path may not always be smooth, but the rewards are worth every step. Start today, trust the process, and create the future you deserve.

Conclusion

As we close this journey together, I want to take a moment to recap the key lessons that have guided my path to financial freedom and can guide yours as well:

1. Start Early

The sooner you begin saving and investing, the more time you give your money to grow. But even if you're starting later, every step forward counts.

2. Stay Consistent

Wealth is built through steady, ongoing contributions. Automate your savings and stick to the plan, no matter what life throws your way.

3. Keep It Simple

You don't need complex strategies to succeed. Low-cost index funds, patience, and discipline are enough to build a secure financial future.

Take the First Step Today

No matter where you are financially — whether you're just starting out, catching up, or looking to optimize your strategy — the most important thing is to take action. Every dollar you save, every investment you make, and every bit of financial knowledge you gain brings you closer to your goals.

Don't wait for the perfect time or ideal circumstances. Start small, start imperfectly, but start today. Remember, time is your best ally, and the earlier you begin, the more you benefit.

A Personal Note of Encouragement

I wrote this book because I believe in you. I know how daunting it can feel to think about saving and investing, especially if you're starting with little or have faced financial challenges. But if my journey has shown me anything, it's that ordinary people can achieve extraordinary things with the right mindset and tools.

You don't need to be wealthy to start, and you don't need to be perfect to succeed. What you need is the courage to begin and the persistence to keep going. I'm rooting for you, and I know that with time, discipline, and faith in yourself, you can create the financial freedom you deserve.

This is your moment. Take that first step, stay the course, and watch as your efforts transform your future. Here's to your success and the incredible journey ahead!

Appendix

Appendix A: Common Mistakes to Avoid

Even with the best intentions, it's easy to make financial mistakes that can derail your progress. Here's a list of common pitfalls and how to avoid them:

1. Timing the Market

- **The Mistake**: Trying to predict market highs and lows to buy or sell at the "right time."
- **Why It's Harmful**: Most people end up buying high and selling low, missing out on the long-term benefits of staying invested.
- **How to Avoid It**: Stick to consistent contributions and ignore short-term market fluctuations. Trust that the market will recover and grow over time.

2. Ignoring Employer Matches

- **The Mistake**: Not contributing enough to your 401(k) to get the full employer match.

- **Why It's Harmful**: This is essentially leaving free money on the table.
- **How to Avoid It**: Always contribute at least enough to get the full employer match—this is one of the simplest ways to accelerate your savings.

3. Carrying High-Interest Debt

- **The Mistake**: Letting credit card balances pile up while paying only the minimum.
- **Why It's Harmful**: High-interest rates can quickly snowball, making it harder to save or invest.
- **How to Avoid It**: Pay off credit card debt as a top priority before focusing on other financial goals.

4. Not Starting Early Enough

- **The Mistake**: Waiting to save or invest because retirement feels far away.
- **Why It's Harmful**: The longer you wait, the less time you give your money to grow through compounding.

- **How to Avoid It**: Start now, even if it's just a small amount. The earlier you begin, the greater your long-term returns.

Appendix B: Quick Start Guide

For readers who want to take action right away, here's a step-by-step guide to get started on your journey to financial freedom:

1. Open a Retirement Account

- Set up a Roth IRA, 401(k), or both.
- If your employer offers a 401(k) match, contribute at least enough to get the full match.

2. Set Up Automatic Contributions

- Automate your savings to ensure consistent contributions, no matter the market conditions.

3. Choose a Low-Cost Index Fund

- Start with a fund like Vanguard S&P 500 or a total stock market index fund.

4. Pay Off High-Interest Debt

- Eliminate credit card balances or other high-interest loans to free up more money for saving and investing.

5. Build an Emergency Fund

- Save three to six months' worth of expenses in a liquid, accessible account to cover unexpected costs.

6. Stay the Course

- Ignore short-term market noise and focus on your long-term goals.

Made in United States
North Haven, CT
04 November 2026

21765030R00053